BRAVE KIDS

Hazelle Boxberg

Susan E. Goodman

Illustrated by Doris Ettlinger

Aladdin Paperbacks
New York London Toronto Sydney

First Aladdin Paperbacks edition February 2004
Text copyright © 2004 by Susan E. Goodman
Illustrations copyright © 2004 by Doris Ettlinger

ALADDIN PAPERBACKS
An imprint of Simon & Schuster
Children's Publishing Division
1230 Avenue of the Americas
New York, NY 10020

Also available in an Aladdin Library edition.
Designed by Debra Sfetsios
The text of this book was set in Palatino.

Printed in the United States of America
2 4 6 8 10 9 7 5 3 1
Library of Congress Control Number 2003106433

ISBN 13: 978-0-689-84982-4
ISBN 10: 0-689-84982-6

Table of Contents

Chapter One
November 1918   I

Chapter Two
All Aboard the Orphan Train   8

Chapter Three
The Ride to Texas   15

Chapter Four
Up on Stage   23

Chapter Five
Dr. Nelson's House   30

Chapter Six
Night Flight   36

Chapter Seven
Another Chance   42

Chapter Eight
"I Am Not an Orphan!"   47

Afterword
Hazelle Boxberg Latimer, 1907–1997 54

Further Reading   60

To Debbie—who has helped lift
many a girl's spirit

Acknowledgments

Thanks to Edward Gray, who introduced me to Hazelle
in his wonderful documentary, *The Orphan Trains*; Carol
Taylor of the W. Walworth Harrison Public Library, who
acquainted me with her town of Greenville, Texas; and
Elizabeth Tredway, who shared her memories of "Aunt
Hazelle." A special thanks to the founder of the Orphan
Train Heritage Society of America, Mary Ellen Johnson,
who was very generous with her time and resources.

Thanks to reader Deborah Hirschland for all of her
invaluable insights. To Doris Ettlinger, whose illustrations add so much to the story. And to Molly McGuire
and Ellen Krieger, who are always there, always helpful.

Chapter One

November 1918

The grown-ups were out of the dining room. It was time for some fun.

Johnny made his monkey face for Emma. But Mildred was the one who laughed. She giggled so hard that George was able to steal the bread off her plate.

Hazelle didn't join in. She was thinking about the last time she saw Mama.

It had been January 7. Hazelle had been in her fourth-grade classroom. Mama had come to the door. She was carrying a suitcase for Hazelle.

"I just went to the doctor," Mama said. "He wants me to go to the hospital. They'll find out why I have such bad headaches."

Mama looked into Hazelle's worried eyes. She smiled softly.

"I'll be back soon," she said.

Then she touched Hazelle's cheek.

"Stand tall, my sweet girl," she whispered. "And be strong."

Hazelle had thought Mama would be back in a few days. That was months ago. Now Hazelle was in the Grace Home. It was an orphanage in New York City.

It's been almost a year since I've seen her, Hazelle thought. *It feels like forever.*

Mrs. Miller came to the doorway. Mrs. Miller was in charge of the orphanage. A tall woman stood beside her.

"Children!" Mrs. Miller called. She clapped her hands twice to get their attention.

The noise brought Hazelle out of her dreams and back into the orphanage.

"It's time to clear your plates," Mrs. Miller said. "Then on to evening chores.

"I need to talk to some of you," she continued. "If I tap your shoulder, you will stay behind."

Mrs. Miller marched to the table. Hazelle was the very first one she touched.

What have I done? Hazelle wondered. *Am I going to get in trouble?*

The matron didn't say a word. She kept walking around the table.

Next she tapped Johnny O'Neil. That

scared Hazelle even more. Johnny was always being punished.

Then Mrs. Miller leaned over little Emma. She gently brushed Emma's blond bangs off her forehead.

"Emma, you stay too," she said.

Emma is only three, thought Hazelle. *She couldn't have done anything wrong. What's going on?*

Hazelle scooped Emma into her lap. She watched Mrs. Miller finish picking her group. Hazelle rubbed Emma's soft hair with her cheek.

"Children, this is Miss Comstock," Mrs. Miller said. "She works for the Children's Aid Society. She has good news for you."

The tall woman stepped closer. As she did the feathers on her hat bobbed up and down.

"You are very lucky children," she said. "You are going on a trip."

Miss Comstock explained that the next few days would be very busy. Each child would be given new clothes and a new suitcase. On Tuesday they would go to the train station.

"You're going on a long train ride," she told them. "You are going all the way to Texas."

"What is Texas?" asked Emma.

"Texas is your new home," said Miss Comstock. "That's where we're going to find new families for all of you."

Some children started to clap. Others laughed out loud.

Emma didn't really understand what was happening. But she saw how excited everyone was. She hopped off Hazelle's lap and began skipping around the room.

"Going to Texas. Going to Texas," Emma chanted.

Hazelle sat very still for a minute. Then she spoke up.

"I can't go," she said. "My mother is still alive. I am not an orphan."

Chapter Two

All Aboard the Orphan Train

"All aboard!" the train conductor shouted.

The orphans were already on the train. They sat in pairs on the hard benches. Each older child had a little one to care for.

Miss Comstock sat near them. Another woman from the Children's Aid Society was with her. Her name was Miss Hill. Miss Hill held baby William in her arms.

The children were wearing their new clothes. Johnny kept brushing off his knickers.

Emma loved her gloves. She would not take them off.

There were fourteen children in all—including Hazelle.

Hazelle was not excited about her new clothes. In fact, she felt so angry she wanted to cry. But she didn't. Things were happening so fast.

Hazelle had tried talking to Miss Comstock.

"I am not an orphan," she had said over and over.

Miss Comstock would not change her mind. She just kept saying the same thing—"You're going to Texas."

So here I am, Hazelle thought.

Then she remembered her mother's words. "Stand tall, my sweet girl," Mama had said. "And be strong."

"Hazelle, you're eleven years old. Stand

tall," Hazelle whispered to herself.

She straightened up in her seat. Then she turned to Emma. Hazelle was Emma's "little mother" on the trip.

"Snuggle up, Emma," she said. "I'll tell you a story."

Just then the train had its own story to tell. The whistle blew its last warning. A few jolts and they were off.

The 1,500-mile journey to Greenville, Texas, had begun.

The children jumped up to look out their windows. They watched the train station get smaller and smaller.

Hazelle pressed her face against the glass. She watched New York City pass by. She tried to memorize every building.

Soon the train reached the country. Emma pointed out the window.

"Look, Hazelle, a pink dog!" she said.

Hazelle smiled. "That isn't a dog, you silly goose," she said. "That's a pig."

"Oink," said Mildred, leaning over the top of Hazelle and Emma's bench.

"Oink," said Emma. "Oink, oink."

"Ever seen a pig before?" Mildred asked Hazelle.

"In books," Hazelle answered.

"Do you think we're going to live on farms with pigs?" Mildred whispered.

Hazelle shrugged. She wasn't going to worry about that now.

Instead she and Emma counted pigs. They played pat-a-cake. Then Hazelle started to sing her a song.

"Shhh!" Miss Hill said. "Just whispering, girls."

Hazelle looked at Mildred and rolled her

eyes. But she did quiet down. She and Emma played finger games.

Meanwhile Miss Hill asked Mildred to pass out dinner. She gave each child a bologna sandwich.

A woman nearby stood up. She had been watching the children. Hazelle had seen her chuckle during Emma's oinking concert.

"These children are orphans, aren't they?" she asked Miss Hill.

"Yes," Miss Hill answered.

"I'd like to buy them milk to go with their supper," the woman said.

Miss Hill frowned.

"No, thank you," she said. "Milk might make them queasy. They can drink water."

The woman walked back to her seat. She caught Hazelle's eye. Her little smile said, *I'm sorry,* without saying a word.

Hazelle swallowed her anger at Miss Hill along with her sandwich. She walked Emma to the water fountain. She helped her drink from the paper cup.

"I'm tired," Emma complained on the way back.

Hazelle sat on the bench. She patted her leg. "Put your head here," she said. "I'm your pillow tonight."

Emma stretched out. Hazelle stroked her hair. Soon Emma fell asleep.

Hazelle looked out the window. It was getting dark outside—inside, too. Dusk was turning into night.

Hazelle listened to the train chugging along.

Going to Texas, going to Texas, it sang to her.

Hazelle listened to it for hours.

Chapter Three

The Ride to Texas

Johnny passed out more sandwiches.

"Bologna again?" asked Emma.

"Again and again and again," said Hazelle.

Bologna sandwiches for dinner, then breakfast, lunch, and dinner once more.

Hazelle looked at her sandwich. The bread was getting hard. The edges of the meat were curling up.

Mildred peeked over the bench.

"These sandwiches are as tired as we are," she said.

Hazelle and Mildred giggled quietly. It had been another long day on the train.

A man leaving the car heard them.

"You two have a good sense of humor," he said. "I just finished my newspaper. Would you like the funnies?"

"Yes, please," Hazelle replied.

Hazelle opened the newspaper. Emma snuggled close. Mildred put her chin on the top of their bench.

Hazelle began reading a comic where a farmer kicks a horse.

"That man is too mean," Emma said.

"Let's see what comes next," said Hazelle.

She showed Emma the rest of the pictures.

"All at once a big storm blows up," said

Hazelle. "The horse is swept up by the wind. Look, it's thrown on top of the farmer."

"Serves that farmer right!" Mildred exclaimed.

"Are there big storms in Texas?" asked Emma.

"Don't worry," said Hazelle. "Horses only fall on mean farmers. Let's read *Mutt and Jeff.*"

All three girls laughed at that one. Hazelle had begun the next comic when Johnny came over.

"Sorry, Hazelle," he said. "Miss Comstock said you must be quiet. I have to bring the paper to her."

Talk about someone being too mean, Hazelle thought.

"Come on, Emma, let's get some water," she said. She took the little girl's hand.

17

The conductor walked by the water fountain.

"How are my favorite girls?" he asked.

"I'm fine," said Hazelle. She didn't really feel fine. But he was a nice man for asking.

"I'm three," said Emma.

The conductor smiled.

"You are also lucky," he said. "I've been putting the new passengers in another car. Now we have empty seats in this one. You'll sleep much better tonight."

The conductor started moving the orphans around. Soon there was a whole bench for each of them. They could all stretch out for the night.

My knees are happy, at least, thought Hazelle.

The children settled down. One by one they all fell asleep.

Hours later the brakes squealed. The train jolted to a stop. The lights in the car came on. The children sat up and looked around.

Hazelle's friend the conductor rushed through the car.

"Why did we stop?" Hazelle asked him.

"We're crossing the Mason-Dixon line," he answered.

Before Hazelle could ask what that meant, he was gone.

"Look at all those colored people, Hazelle," said Emma.

Hazelle tried to hush the little girl. Emma stared as lines of Negroes streamed through the car.

"Did they forget to buy tickets?" whispered Emma. Emma's whisper was so loud that everyone could hear.

One man stopped. He stood right in front of Emma.

"No, missy," he said, "we all have tickets . . . just like you."

Then he walked on.

Finally the parade of people ended. Another traveler caught Hazelle's eye. She wiggled her finger, telling Hazelle and Emma to come over.

"The train crossed the Mason-Dixon line," she whispered. "That means we're in the southern part of the country.

"In the South colored people must ride in a separate car," she said.

"Back in your seats, girls," ordered Miss Comstock. "The lights are about to go off."

Hazelle boosted Emma back onto her bench. She tucked her in, using her coat as a blanket. Then she settled in herself.

The train started up. The lights went out again.

I feel sorry for those people, Hazelle thought. *I know how it feels to be forced to go where you don't want to be.*

Chapter Four

Up on Stage

"Button your jacket, Johnny," Miss Comstock said. "Hazelle, tie Emma's shoe. Herman, wipe that dirt off your cheek."

After three days on the train the children were in Greenville, Texas. They were at the Beckham Hotel.

They were also very tired. But they had washed up. They had put on their other new clothes.

"Signs have been up all over town," said

23

Miss Comstock. "So people who want children will be at the Masonic Hall today.

"We're ready to go there now," she said.

"Be polite," Miss Hill told them. "Answer all their questions."

Miss Comstock bent down to talk to the youngest orphans.

"Emma, Herman, if a lady talks to you, take her hand," she said. "Tell her you want a new mommy."

Nobody better try that with me, thought Hazelle.

"Children, line up in pairs," Miss Comstock ordered.

Hazelle took Emma's hand. She gave it a squeeze. Then the group walked out of the hotel.

Hazelle saw all the buggies and cars in front of the hall. Her heart started beating very fast. She looked at little Emma.

She's so young and pretty, Hazelle thought. *Maybe someone will take us both.*

Miss Hill held the door open.

"Let's go," said Miss Comstock. She walked inside.

"Smile," whispered Miss Hall to the children as they passed her. "Remember to smile."

Hazelle held Emma's hand even tighter. She didn't feel like smiling.

"Look, Hazelle," said Emma. "There are so many people here."

Hazelle didn't feel like looking, either. She kept her eyes on Miss Comstock.

The children walked onto the stage. That's when Hazelle peeked around the room. Everyone was looking at them!

Hazelle remembered going to the zoo with her mother. Now she knew how the

animals felt. She felt like she was in a cage.

Miss Comstock made a short speech. Then people came up to meet the children.

A woman walked up to Johnny. She squeezed his arms.

"He seems strong enough," she said.

Suddenly Hazelle realized that Emma was no longer beside her.

"Emma?" Hazelle called softly. "Emma . . ."

Then she stopped. Hazelle saw Emma near a lady wearing a red hat. The woman's soft eyes reminded her of Mama's.

The lady took Emma's hand.

"Would you like to come home with me?" she asked Emma.

Emma nodded shyly.

The pair began walking toward Miss Comstock. Hazelle caught Emma's eye. She blew Emma a kiss.

Then she felt a tap on her shoulder. Hazelle turned to see a man standing in front of her. His jacket was dirty.

"Let's take a look at you," the man said. "Turn around a few times."

Hazelle turned very slowly.

The man came even closer. Hazelle didn't like the way he smelled.

"Open your mouth," the man said.

Hazelle just looked at him. Why did he want her to do that?

"Open your mouth," he said again. "I want to see if you have good teeth."

Hazelle slowly opened her mouth. The man stuck his finger inside. He rubbed her teeth to feel if they were strong.

Hazelle wanted to bite his hand. She wanted to run away. She didn't do either.

Please go away, she begged silently.

Finally the man moved on. All the air rushed out of Hazelle's lungs. She hadn't even known that she was holding her breath.

Hazelle looked around the room. Emma was gone. Herman was with a couple and their four children. Mildred was walking out with a family too. She crossed her fingers for luck and held them up for Hazelle to see.

Hazelle felt confused. She didn't want a new family. But why didn't anyone want her?

Just then Miss Comstock came over to her.

"Hazelle," she said, "you are going home with Dr. Nelson."

Chapter Five

Dr. Nelson's House

The ride to Dr. Nelson's house was short—and quiet. Dr. Nelson wasn't one much for talking.

Hazelle didn't know what to say anyway. So she listened to the *clip-clop* of the horse pulling their buggy.

She also peeked at Dr. Nelson when he wasn't looking. He was a small man. Gray hair curled underneath his hat.

He looks a hundred years old, she thought.

The doctor pulled up to a neat white house. He tied the horse to a post. An old lady stood in the doorway.

"Well, you look all right," she said.

All right for what? Hazelle wondered.

"We've already had our supper," she said. "But I'll put out food for you two."

While Mrs. Nelson filled two plates, a younger woman came into the kitchen.

"I'm Sarah," she said. "I'm married to John, the Nelsons' son."

Sarah gave Hazelle a warm smile. It helped melt Hazelle's fear.

Dr. Nelson ate without saying a word. Mrs. Nelson swept up a few crumbs that had fallen on the floor. She scrubbed a counter that already looked clean.

Sarah sat near Hazelle. She asked about her trip.

She seems nice, thought Hazelle between answers and bites of dinner.

Sarah told Hazelle that her husband was a soldier. He was stationed far away in Virginia.

"I'm so happy the war is over," said Sarah. "Soon my Johnny will be home. I can't wait to see him."

"Pie, Hazelle?" asked Mrs. Nelson. She cut a big piece and put it on Hazelle's plate. She set a large glass of milk down as well.

Then she quickly washed the knife she'd used.

The Nelsons seem nice too, Hazelle thought. *Old and fussy, but nice.*

Later that night Hazelle changed her mind.

She was upstairs. She was in the bedroom she would share with Sarah. She was reaching for her nightgown.

Sarah came in and closed the door. She sat on the bed. Then she patted the spot next to her. Hazelle sat down too.

"Hazelle, you seem like such a nice girl," Sarah said. "I have to tell you the truth."

She put her arm around Hazelle's shoulder.

"I told you that my husband is coming back soon," said Sarah. "When he does, we'll be moving on.

"The Nelsons are getting older," Sarah continued. "You are young. But you are old enough to clean house.

"I'm sorry to tell you this," said Sarah. "Dr. Nelson went to the hall today just to find someone to take care of them."

Hazelle slumped against Sarah. But at that moment she felt totally alone.

Oh, Mama, where are you? she thought sadly.

Stand tall and be strong, Mama answered.

Hazelle sat up. She looked straight at Sarah.

"Miss Comstock is still at the hotel," she said.

"You must go tell her you cannot stay here," Sarah said.

"How do I get back?" Hazelle asked.

"It's not that far," Sarah answered. "I'll draw you a map. You can sneak out after dark. There's a full moon tonight, so you'll be able to find your way."

Hazelle put her things back in her suitcase. She tied her shoes. Then she sat back on the bed.

Sarah took her hand. They waited for the moon to rise. It would light up Hazelle's escape—back to the Beckham Hotel.

Chapter Six

Night Flight

Hazelle checked her map one more time. She traced the route with her finger.

I'm almost there, she thought. *Turn onto Oak Street. Then go all the way to Lee.*

Sarah was right. The full moon did give off a lot of light. But it was still nighttime.

Hazelle kept her eyes on the road ahead of her. She tried not to feel scared or alone.

She tried not to think about what Dr. Nelson's face would look like when he discovered she was gone. Or Miss Comstock's reaction when she saw Hazelle again.

Ah-oo-oooo. A loud cry echoed through the street. It chased all other thoughts from Hazelle's mind.

The second howl filled Hazelle with terror.

What was that? she wondered. *A wolf? A coyote?*

Suddenly the shadows looked very dark and dangerous.

Do they have coyotes in Texas? she wondered. *Do coyotes eat people?*

Ah-oo. Ah-oo-oooo. The sound was getting louder.

Hazelle began to shiver.

Will it chase me if I start to run? she asked herself.

The next yowl made Hazelle's decision for her. She dashed down the road.

The animal was getting closer. Hazelle could hear its claws clicking on the road. She picked up speed.

Suddenly Hazelle's suitcase hit her leg. The suitcase went flying. So did Hazelle. She fell onto the ground.

She quickly rolled over to face her enemy.

And she saw that enemy wagging its tail.

"A dog!" she exclaimed. "Just an old yellow dog!"

Hazelle was so relieved she laughed out loud. She got up. The dog came over and nudged her with his nose.

Hazelle scratched between his ears.

"Want to keep me company?" she asked. "Protect me from all those Texas coyotes?"

"Lucky," a voice called out in the darkness. "Lucky, come home."

Lucky gave Hazelle one last lick. Then he trotted off.

Hazelle watched the dog go into a house nearby. Light was pouring through its doorway. Hazelle could see a group of people inside.

Looks like a real family, she thought. *A family with a yellow dog.*

"Hey, Ma," a boy in the house called out. "There's a girl in the road."

Hazelle froze. She felt nailed to her spot.

A woman walked onto the porch.

"Is something wrong, young lady?" she asked. "Do you need help?"

Hazelle's moment of surprise was over. She grabbed her suitcase. Once again she began to run.

I'm almost there, she thought. *Go down Oak*

Street, turn right on Lee. Keep going till the Beckham Hotel.

Hazelle dashed through the hotel lobby. She ran right to Miss Comstock's room. She pounded on the door.

"Who is it?" asked Miss Comstock.

Hazelle didn't wait. She burst into the room.

Miss Comstock sat up in bed. She looked very surprised.

"Hazelle, what on earth are you doing here?" Miss Comstock asked.

"They didn't want a child," Hazelle said. "They wanted a slave."

Chapter Seven

Another Chance

Miss Comstock was reading the newspaper. She was looking out the window. She was looking everywhere—except at Hazelle.

Miss Comstock is really mad, thought Hazelle. *But what else could I do?*

Baby William was sitting on the floor. He wasn't going to his new family until afternoon. Hazelle lay down on the rug beside him.

Hazelle tickled his leg. She liked to hear him laugh.

"You're lucky," she whispered. "You don't remember your mama."

Hazelle started a game of peekaboo. Hiding her eyes, she didn't see the new shadow cast across the floor.

She did hear the knock. Hazelle spun her head around.

A man filled the doorway. He held his hat in his two huge hands.

That's the biggest man I have ever seen, she thought.

"May I come in?" the man asked.

"Of course," said Miss Comstock. "Hazelle is right here on the floor.

"Get up and shake hands, Hazelle," she said.

Hazelle stood up. But she kept her eyes on the floor. All she could see were the man's legs. They were wrapped in overalls washed

so many times that they were soft blue.

Hazelle watched the overalls walk toward her. Then the man's hand reached out and covered hers.

"Pleased to meet you," he said.

He was a big man. But his voice was gentle.

"Mrs. Tredway and I have wanted a daughter for a long time," the man said.

I already am *someone's daughter*, Hazelle thought.

She sneaked a look at Miss Comstock.

The matron's lips were pressed into a straight line. Her face flashed a stern warning.

Hazelle picked at a wrinkle in her dress.

"We want you to be our little girl," he said.

Hazelle did not say a word.

45

Neither did Mr. Tredway. He was waiting.

Hazelle slowly looked up—and up. She wondered if she would ever get to the top of him. He was so tall and strong.

"If you hit me, I will never be able to get up," she said finally.

Mr. Tredway squatted down so he was no taller than Hazelle. His kind eyes looked into hers. They were serious and smiling at the same time.

"My dear," he said, "I promise I will never hit you."

Hazelle looked at Mr. Tredway. She gave him a very little smile.

"Let's go home," he said.

Chapter Eight

"I Am Not an Orphan!"

"Hop in!" said Mr. Tredway.

Hazelle got into Mr. Tredway's motorcar. She sat on the hard black leather.

Mr. Tredway walked to the front of the automobile. He turned its crank. The engine began to putter.

Mr. Tredway climbed in too. His head brushed against the car's canvas top.

"Next stop—your new home," he said.

Hazelle just looked out the window. She

watched the Beckham Hotel disappear once more. Soon they were out in the country.

It would be harder to get back to the hotel this time, Hazelle thought.

As he drove Mr. Tredway pointed out farms where children her age lived.

"These fields look cold and sad now," he said. "But wait until the cotton is ready for picking. It looks like snow in summertime!"

Will I be here next summer? Hazelle wondered.

Mr. Tredway told her that he and his wife had a son named Hugh. But they wanted a daughter too.

"We like having laughter in our house," he said.

Every so often Mr. Tredway glanced over at Hazelle. He didn't seem to mind that Hazelle was so quiet. He kept on talking.

"Ever been around animals?" he asked.

This time Hazelle had an answer.

"Mama took me to the zoo once," she said proudly. "We saw tigers and elephants."

"That must have been a sight," he said, smiling. "No tigers on our farm, although Hugh would surely like that idea.

"We do have chickens and horses," he continued. "And soon I just might teach you how to milk a cow."

That might be fun, Hazelle thought.

Mr. Tredway turned into a yard. He honked the horn a few times.

"Willie, we're here!" he called.

A woman came out of the farmhouse. She was wiping her hands on her apron. She walked over to the car.

"Hello there," she said. She gave Hazelle a big smile of welcome.

"She's a pretty little thing," the woman said to her husband.

"Come take a look inside, Hazelle," said Mr. Tredway.

Mr. Tredway picked up Hazelle's suitcase. He and his wife started back toward the house.

Hazelle began to follow them. A picture of Mama flashed into her mind.

It's now or never, she thought.

"I am not an orphan," Hazelle said.

"I am not an orphan!" she said much louder.

Mr. and Mrs. Tredway stopped walking. They turned to face her. Their eyes were filled with questions.

"My mother is not dead," Hazelle said. And the rest of her story came pouring out.

Mrs. Tredway looked surprised when she

heard Mama had been in the hospital so long. She added up the months in her mind. She put a hand on Hazelle's shoulder.

"You must miss your mama very much," she said.

"Oh yes, ma'am," said Hazelle.

Mr. and Mrs. Tredway looked at each other for a long time. Then Mrs. Tredway gave a tiny nod.

Mr. Tredway squatted down so Hazelle could see his face. He wanted her to know that he meant every word.

"Hazelle, we'll find out what happened to your mama," he said. "We'll drive to Greenville tomorrow to talk to Miss Comstock. We'll write a letter to the hospital.

"Meanwhile, you need someone to take care of you," he said. "We'd like to try."

Hazelle had been holding back her tears

for a long time. They sprang into her eyes again.

But this time she didn't feel angry. She felt hopeful.

Mrs. Tredway saw those tears. She gently dried them with her apron.

"Let's go in, Hazelle," she said. "I'm making a patchwork quilt for your bed. There's still time to add some of your favorite colors."

Mrs. Tredway put her arm around Hazelle's shoulder. And they slowly walked toward the door.

Hazelle Boxberg Latimer, 1907–1997

This is a true story.

Hazelle Boxberg was a real girl. She really lived in an orphanage after her mother got sick. She really rode an orphan train with Emma. And read the funnies and ate bologna sandwiches and crossed the Mason-Dixon line. She really left the doctor's home and lived with the Tredways.

Eventually Mr. Tredway learned that Hazelle's mother was still in the hospital.

She was very sick. Hazelle was able to write her a few letters before she died.

Hazelle stayed with the Tredways. She came to love "Dad" Tredway very much. She lived in their caring home until she grew up.

As the author of this book, I tried to stick to the facts. I did make up parts of the story I didn't know, like Dr. Nelson's last name and the name of the woman at the Grace Home. I also added some of Hazelle's private thoughts. And since I didn't know what happened during Hazelle's nighttime escape, I imagined it.

Of course, orphan trains really existed. Today the idea of sending children across the country to live with strangers seems mean. Back then it seemed like a good way to deal with a difficult problem.

In the 1850s life in America's big cities

could be very hard. Many families came there from other countries without much money. Parents couldn't always find work. Many died from diseases like flu or yellow fever.

At that time 500,000 people lived in New York City. About 30,000 of them were homeless children. These children slept outside in doorways and old boxes. Some sold rags or matches to earn money for food. Others became thieves.

Social workers wanted these children to have better lives. They decided to find families for them out west. Life on a farm seemed better than life on the streets.

The first orphan train left New York in 1854. Many more followed. Like Hazelle, many children on them were not orphans. Sometimes a mother had died and the father

couldn't care for his children. Sometimes parents gave their children up, hoping their lives would improve. The orphan trains continued until 1929. By then about 250,000 children had gone west.

Before each trip notices were placed in a town's newspaper—WANTED: HOMES FOR CHILDREN. The children were supposed to become real family members. They were to be sent to school. Agents like Miss Comstock were supposed to visit them to make sure all was well.

Many of these children's stories had happy endings. Orphans often felt that their lives were saved. But not always. Some orphans were unloved or abused. As Hazelle said, some families "didn't want a child. They wanted a slave."

Emma was very happy. A young couple

adopted her. They loved her as their own little girl.

In 1990 Emma read a newspaper article about orphan trains. She found Hazelle's telephone number. They lived only ten miles apart. Yet they hadn't seen each other since that day at the Masonic Hall. Emma (whose new parents had changed her name to Helen) called Hazelle. They became good friends again. They stayed friends until the day Hazelle died.

Further Reading

If you liked reading about Hazelle and orphan trains, you can also try:

Bunting, Eve. *Train to Somewhere.*
New York: Clarion Books, 1996.

Nixon, Joan Lowery. *A Family Apart.*
New York: Random House, 1996.

Warren, Andrea. *Orphan Train Rider: One Boy's True Story.*
Boston: Houghton Mifflin, 1996.

Warren, Andrea. *We Rode the Orphan Trains.*
Boston: Houghton Mifflin, 2001.

9 780689 849824

Made in the USA
Middletown, DE
27 August 2018